Salad Renaissance

1500 Days of Crisp and Inspired Salad Recipes to Revitalize Your Palate | Full Color Edition

Elizabeth E. Wright

Copyright© 2024 By Elizabeth E. Wright Rights Reserved

This book is copyright protected. It is only for personal use. You cannot amend, distribute, sell, use, quote or paraphrase any part of the content within this book, without the consent of the author or publisher.

Under no circumstances will any blame or legal responsibility be held against the publisher, or author, for any damages, reparation, or monetary loss due to the information contained within this book, either directly or indirectly.

Disclaimer Notice:

Please note the information contained within this document is for educational and entertainment purposes only. All effort has been executed to present accurate, up to date, reliable, complete information. No warranties of any kind are declared or implied. Readers acknowledge that the author is not engaged in the rendering of legal, financial, medical or professional advice. The content within this book has been derived from various sources. Please consult a licensed professional before attempting any techniques outlined in this book.

By reading this document, the reader agrees that under no circumstances is the author responsible for any losses, direct or indirect, that are incurred as a result of the use of the information contained within this document, including, but not limited to, errors, omissions, or inaccuracies.

Editor: AALIYAH LYONS

Cover Art: DANIELLE REES

Interior Design: BROOKE WHITE

Food stylist: Sienna Adams

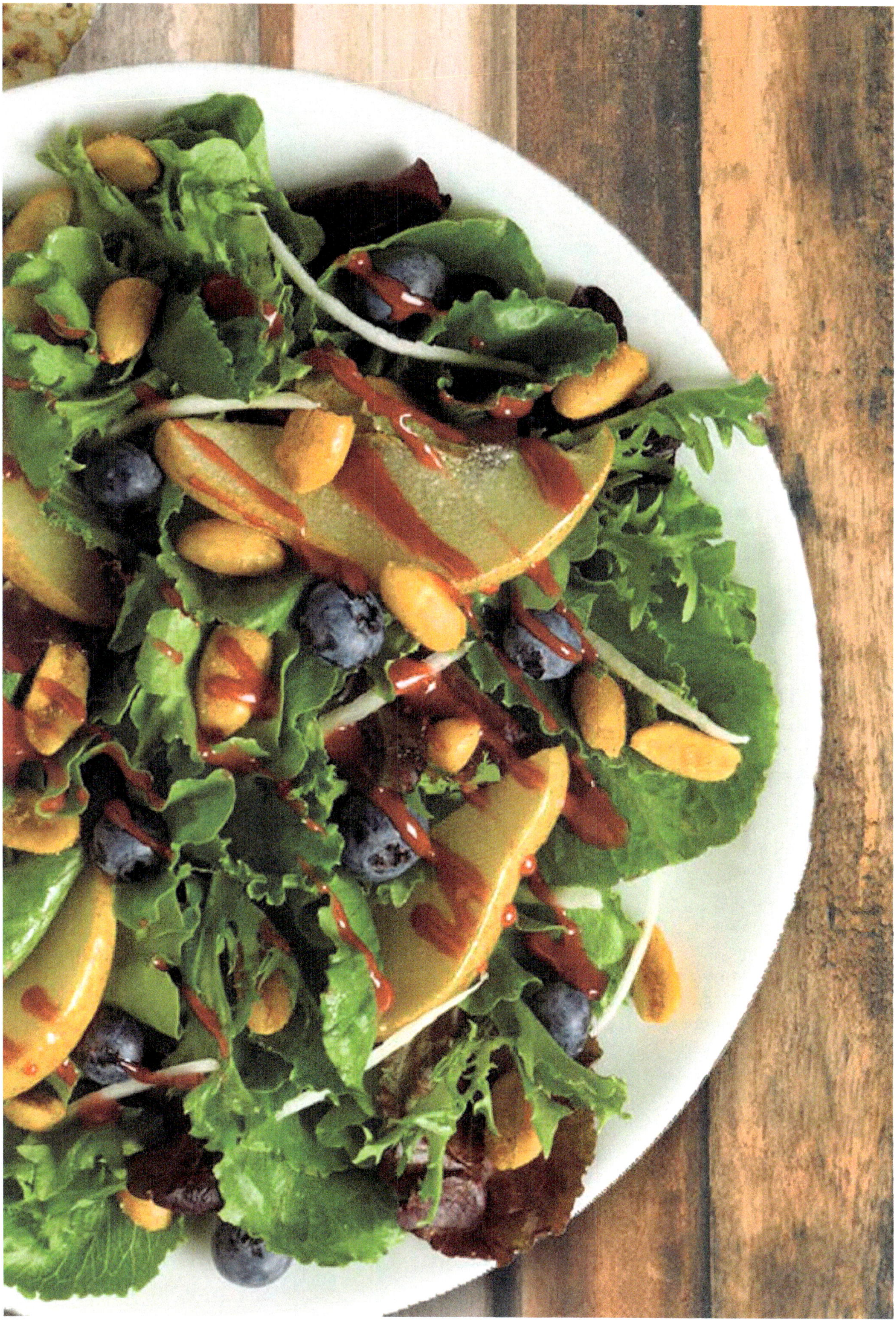

Table Of Contents

Introduction — 1

Chapter 1
The Well-Equipped Salad Kitchen — 2
Must-Have Equipment for Salad Aficionados — 3
From Fridge to Salad Bowl — 4
A Journey Through Seasons — 5

Chapter 2
Flavorful Dressings — 8
Basic Vinaigrette — 9
Lemon Cashew Dressing — 9
Balsamic Maple Vinaigrette — 10
Herb Vinaigrette — 10
Dijon & Tarragon Dressing — 11
Creamy Avocado Lime Dressing — 11
Raw Zucchini Hummus — 12
Greek Yogurt Ranch Dressing — 12
Lemon Vinaigrette — 13
Ginger-Miso Vinaigrette — 13
Caesar-Style Dressing — 14

Roasted Garlic Dressing — 14

Chapter 3
Vibrant Vegetable Salads and Slaws — 15
Horiatiki Greek Country Salad — 16
Sweet Sesame Edamame Slaw — 16
Russian Potato Salad — 17
Potato and Broccoli Salad — 17
Fiesta Chili-Lime Mixed Greens Avocado Salad — 18
Spinach and Almonds Salad — 18
Waldorf Salad — 19
Italian Sub Salad — 19
Bountiful Seaweed Salad — 20
Detox Red Cabbage Kale Slaw — 20
Cucumber and Onion Quinoa Salad — 21
Caramelized Onion and Beet Salad — 21

Chapter 4
Wholesome Grain, Bean, and Pasta Salads — 22
Italian Bean and Rice Salad — 23

Farro Grape Salad	23
Spiced Lentil Salad	24
Mexican Pasta Salad	24
Corn Bread and Bacon Salad	25
Kale Pesto Pasta Salad	25
Curried Pasta Salad	26
Tomato-Ramen Salad	26
Greek Pasta Salad	27
Green Brown Rice Salad	27
Garden Pasta Salad	28
The Daily Salad	29
Mediterranean Grain Salad	29

Chapter 5
Tasty Tofu and Egg Salads — 30

Vegan Smoked Tofu Salad	31
Summer Cucumber Egg Salad	31
Cold Carrot Tofu Salad	32
Chilled Miso Tofu, Cucumber, and Radish Salad	32
BBQ Tofu and Quinoa Salad	33
Teriyaki Snow Pea Tofu Salad	33
Classic Egg Salad	34
Avocado Egg Salad	34
Mashed Potato Salad with Eggs	35
Sesame Ginger Tofu Salad	35
Creamy Potato and Tofu Salad	36
Tofu "Egg" Salad	36
Hearty Chopped Salad	37
Bistro Breakfast Salad	37

Chapter 6
Fresh Fish and Seafood Salads — 38

Shrimp and Peas Pasta Salad	39
Mediterranean Quinoa-Salmon Salad	39
Honey Chipotle Fire Shrimp Salad	40
Smoked Salmon and Egg Salad	40
Lobster and Egg Salad	41
Lunchbox Tuna Chickpea Salad	41
Tuna and Cannellini Bean Salad	42
Shrimp Cobb Salad	42
Classic Shrimp and Avocado Salad	43
Grilled Salmon Caesar Salad	43
Smoked Salmon and Yam Salad	44
Hot-And-Sour Salmon Salad	44
Asian Tuna, Snow Pea, and Broccoli Salad	45
Warm Salmon and Potato Salad	45

Chapter 7
Scrumptious Chicken Salads — 46

Asparagus Chicken Salad	47
Chicken Orange Salad	47
Chicken Salad with Mandarin Dressing	48
Greek Chicken Salad	48
Everyday Greek Chicken Salad	49
Fajita Chicken and Pepper Salad	49
Mango Avocado Chicken Salad	50
Barbecue Chicken Pizza Salad	50
Apple and Raisins Chicken Salad	51
Grilled Chicken Caesar Salad	51
Polynesian Chicken Salad	52
Fruity Chicken Chopped Salad	52
Curry Chicken Salad	53
Warm Chicken Salad	53

Chapter 8
Savory Meat Salads — 54

Walnuts and Bacon Salad Greens	55
Blackberry, Ham, and Fig Salad	55
Peach and Pork Salad Rolls	56
Turkey and Cranberry Quinoa Salad	56
Sausage Onion Salad	57
Hawaiian Luau Pork Salad	57
Cold Lamb Salad	58
Steak and Blue Cheese Salad	58
Flank Steak and Peach Salad	
Hot Beef and Broccoli Salad	59
Beef Taco Salad	59
Sizzling Pork Greek Salad	60
Easy Beef Salad Wraps	60

Appendix 1 Measurement Conversion Chart — 61
Appendix 2 The Dirty Dozen and Clean Fifteen — 62
Appendix 3 Index — 64

Introduction

In the realm of gastronomy, where innovation dances with tradition, and flavors weave tales of indulgence, there exists a culinary revolution – the Salad Renaissance. This cookbook, a tribute to the vibrancy and ingenuity of salads, beckons you to embark on a tantalizing journey through a garden of flavors.

Picture a world where salads cease to be mere accompaniments, and instead, they emerge as captivating creations, tantalizing the taste buds and captivating the eye. "Salad Renaissance" is an ode to this transformation, an invitation to explore the depths of salad artistry, and a guide to crafting salads that transcend the ordinary.

within these pages, you'll discover a kaleidoscope of recipes that blur the lines between health and indulgence. Each dish is a masterpiece, carefully curated to embrace the finest produce, textures, and flavors, transforming a simple salad into a culinary revelation. Whether you're a seasoned chef or an aspiring home cook, these recipes are designed to unleash your creativity, inviting you to become the maestro of your salad symphony.

This cookbook is not just about nourishment; it's a celebration of the senses. It challenges the notion that salads are predictable or mundane, offering instead a palette of possibilities. From crisp greens to exotic fruits, from the crunch of nuts to the creaminess of cheeses – "Salad Renaissance" is an exploration of diverse ingredients that harmonize to create extraordinary culinary experiences.

So, let the Salad Renaissance unfold before you. As you leaf through these pages, may you be inspired to reimagine salads as more than just a dish but as an adventure. Here's to a culinary odyssey that transforms everyday greens into extraordinary feasts. Prepare to be captivated, delighted, and, above all, inspired.

Bon appétit!!

Chapter 1

The Well-Equipped Salad Kitchen

Must-Have Equipment for Salad Aficionados

Salads, often celebrated for their simplicity, become culinary masterpieces when crafted with the right tools. If you're a salad aficionado, having the right equipment can transform your kitchen into a salad haven. From efficient chopping to creative presentations, here's a guide to the must-have equipment that will elevate your salad craftsmanship.

QUALITY SALAD SPINNER: SPIN YOUR GREENS TO PERFECTION

A quality salad spinner is a game-changer for any salad enthusiast. Efficiently removing excess water from your greens ensures a crisp and dry base for your salads. Look for a spinner with a sturdy build, easy operation, and ample capacity. The investment in a good salad spinner pays off in the texture and presentation of your salads.

CHEF'S KNIFE: YOUR SALAD'S BEST FRIEND

A sharp, reliable chef's knife is indispensable when it comes to salad preparation. From chopping vegetables to slicing through proteins, a high-quality knife streamlines the entire process. Invest in a knife that feels comfortable in your hand and maintains its sharpness for precise and efficient cutting.

MANDOLINE SLICER: PRECISION AT YOUR FINGERTIPS

For those who appreciate uniform slices and julienne cuts, a mandoline slicer is a must. This versatile tool allows you to achieve consistent thickness, enhancing both the visual appeal and texture of your salads. Ensure it comes with adjustable settings and safety features for a seamless slicing experience.

SALAD BOWL SET: ELEVATE YOUR PRESENTATION

Upgrade your salad presentation with a set of aesthetically pleasing salad bowls. Opt for materials like bamboo, acacia, or glass for a touch of elegance. Having a variety of sizes allows you to tailor your presentation to different occasions, from casual family dinners to elegant gatherings.

HERB SCISSORS: EFFORTLESS HERB INFUSIONS

Herbs add layers of flavor to your salads, and herb scissors make incorporating them a breeze. These specialized scissors are designed with multiple blades to efficiently chop fresh herbs directly into your salad bowl. It's a simple yet effective tool for infusing your salads with aromatic goodness.

CITRUS JUICER: SQUEEZE FRESHNESS INTO EVERY BITE

Take your vinaigrettes and dressings to the next level with a citrus juicer. Extracting fresh juice from lemons, limes, or oranges adds a burst of brightness to your salads. Look for a juicer with a sturdy design and easy cleaning to make this process hassle-free.

GRATER/ZESTER: ENHANCE FLAVORS WITH ZEST

A grater or zester is a versatile tool that can add a zing to your salads. Whether it's citrus zest, grated cheese, or nutmeg, this tool allows you to incorporate bold flavors without overwhelming the dish. Choose a grater with different grating options for flexibility in your culinary creations.

MIXING BOWLS WITH LIDS: PREP AND STORE WITH EASE

Invest in a set of mixing bowls with tight-fitting lids to streamline your salad preparation. These bowls are not only useful for tossing your ingredients but also for storing any leftover salads in the refrigerator. Choose a set with a range of sizes for added convenience.

AVOCADO SLICER: TACKLE AVOCADOS LIKE A PRO

For avocado lovers, an avocado slicer is a handy tool. From effortlessly peeling the skin to perfectly slicing the fruit, this gadget ensures you can enjoy avocados in your salads without the mess. It's a small tool that makes a big difference, especially if avocados are a staple in your salad repertoire.

From Fridge to Salad Bowl

SALAD FRIDGE STAPLES:

- Leafy Greens: Keep your fridge stocked with a variety of leafy greens like spinach, arugula, romaine, and kale. These form the base of your salads, providing essential vitamins and a crisp texture.
- Colorful Vegetables: Ensure a rainbow of veggies in your fridge, such as tomatoes, bell peppers, cucumbers, and carrots. These add vibrant colors, flavors, and nutritional value to your salads.
- Fresh Herbs: Elevate your salads with a selection of fresh herbs like basil, cilantro, and mint. They impart aromatic freshness, turning a simple salad into a culinary delight.
- Cheese: Feta, goat cheese, or Parmesan can add a creamy and savory element to salads. Keep these versatile cheeses on hand for a flavor boost.
- Proteins: Store protein options like grilled chicken, boiled eggs, or tofu for a satisfying and filling salad experience. These items turn your salads into a well-balanced meal.

SALAD PANTRY STAPLES:
- Whole Grains: Quinoa, brown rice, or couscous are excellent additions to salads, providing a hearty and nutritious base.
- Canned Legumes: Stock up on canned chickpeas, black beans, or lentils. These are convenient protein sources that add substance to your salads.
- Nuts and Seeds: Almonds, walnuts, sunflower seeds, or pumpkin seeds contribute a delightful crunch and healthy fats to your salads.
- Dried Fruits: Raisins, cranberries, or apricots can lend a sweet and chewy element to your salads, balancing flavors.
- Olive Oil and Vinegar: These classic pantry staples are essential for creating homemade salad dressings. Opt for extra virgin olive oil and a variety of vinegars for diverse flavor profiles.

SALAD SPICE RACK STAPLES:
- Salt and Pepper: The foundation of seasoning, salt, and pepper enhance the overall taste of your salads.
- Garlic Powder and Onion Powder: These add depth and savory notes without the need for chopping fresh garlic or onions.
- Dried Herbs: Oregano, thyme, basil, and rosemary in dried form can be convenient for quick flavor infusion.
- Paprika and Cumin: Spice up your salads with these aromatic spices, bringing warmth and depth to your dishes.
- Dijon Mustard: A versatile condiment, Dijon mustard is a great addition to salad dressings, providing tanginess and complexity.

A Journey Through Seasons

Salads, those vibrant canvases of flavor and nutrition, are not confined to a single season. In the diverse culinary landscape of the United States, each season brings forth a bounty of fresh ingredients, offering salad enthusiasts a year-round palette of flavors and textures. Let's embark on a journey through the seasons, exploring the diverse ingredients that can grace your salad bowl in different parts of the year.

✦ Year-Round Salad Ingredients Chart

SPRING:

Type of Ingredient
Greens: Arugula, Spinach, Watercress
Vegetables: Asparagus, Radishes, Snap Peas
Fruits: Strawberries, Berries, Citrus
Herbs: Mint, Chives
Nuts & Seeds: Almonds, Sunflower Seeds
Cheese: Feta, Goat Cheese
Proteins: Grilled Chicken, Shrimp
Dressing Elements: Lemon, Dijon Mustard
Extras: Avocado, Edamame

SUMMER:

Type of Ingredient
Greens: Romaine, Butter Lettuce, Kale
Vegetables: Tomatoes, Cucumbers, Bell Peppers
Fruits: Berries, Peaches, Watermelon
Herbs: Basil, Cilantro, Dill
Nuts & Seeds: Walnuts, Pine Nuts, Sunflower Seeds
Cheese: Mozzarella, Feta
Proteins: Grilled Salmon, Tofu
Dressing Elements: Balsamic Vinegar, Olive Oil, Honey Mustard
Extras: Corn, Avocado, Edamame

AUTUMN:

Type of Ingredient
Greens: Kale, Chard, Endive
Vegetables: Butternut Squash, Beets, Brussels Sprouts
Fruits: Apples, Pears, Pomegranates
Herbs: Sage, Rosemary
Nuts & Seeds: Pecans, Pumpkin Seeds
Cheese: Gouda, Blue Cheese
Proteins: Roasted Turkey, Chickpeas
Dressing Elements: Apple Cider Vinegar, Maple Syrup
Extras: Cranberries, Pomegranate Seeds

WINTER:

Type of Ingredient
Greens: Kale, Collard Greens, Endive
Vegetables: Roasted Root Vegetables, Brussels Sprouts
Fruits: Citrus Fruits, Apples, Pears
Herbs: Thyme, Oregano
Nuts & Seeds: Almonds, Pecans, Sesame Seeds
Cheese: Parmesan, Goat Cheese
Proteins: Lentils, Rotisserie Chicken
Dressing Elements: Tahini, Mustard, Apple Cider Vinegar
Extras: Roasted Almonds, Cranberries

TIPS FOR YEAR-ROUND SALAD MASTERY

- Embrace Local Produce: Visit farmers' markets or join a community-supported agriculture (CSA) program to access the freshest, locally sourced ingredients each season.
- Diversify Your Greens: Experiment with a variety of greens to keep your salads interesting. Mix delicate lettuces with heartier options like kale or cabbage.
- Play with Textures: Combine crispy, crunchy, and creamy elements to create a satisfying salad experience. Incorporate nuts, seeds, and different textures of fruits and vegetables.
- Incorporate Whole Grains: Add quinoa, farro, or brown rice for a nutritional boost and added substance to your salads.
- Dressings Matter: Experiment with homemade dressings using seasonal herbs, fruits, and flavored oils to complement the ingredients in your salad.

Armed with essential kitchen tools, we've delved into the efficient preparation of salads, turning a collection of ingredients into visually appealing and palate-pleasing masterpieces. The pantry and spice rack have been unveiled as treasure troves, ensuring that every aspiring chef is well-equipped to transform salads into delightful culinary experiences.

In this odyssey, the kitchen transforms into a stage for creative expression. As we conclude, let the spirit of experimentation guide your salad creations. " Salad Renaissance" is an invitation to revel in the joy of crafting dishes that not only tantalize the taste buds but also celebrate the beauty of each season. May your salads reflect your passion for good food, and may your culinary journey be a perpetual source of inspiration and innovation. Cheers to the art of salad crafting and the countless flavorful adventures that lie ahead!

Chapter 2

Flavorful Dressings

Basic Vinaigrette

Prep time: 5 minutes | Cook time: none | Serves 4

- 2 part cold pressed olive oil (or 1 part olive and 1 part flaxseed oil)
- 1 part apple cider vinegar
- 1 clove garlic, crushed
- Optional: Add some Dijon or grain mustard (for a single salad amount add 1/2 tsp mild mustard)

DRESSING RECOMMENDATIONS

1. Add more oil But remember flavors dilute when you add them to the salad!
2. The other 'fix' that's handy to keep in mind: If you like the consistency and add a very small amount of agave or honey.

BASIL BASIC

3. To the "Basic Vinaigrette" add a handful of basil leaves and blend.

Lemon Cashew Dressing

Prep time: 5 minutes | Cook time: none | Serves 4

- 1/2 cup cashews, soaked (about one hour) and drained
- 1 garlic clove
- 2 tbsp lemon juice
- 2 tbsp olive oil or other
- 1 date, pitted and soaked for 20 minutes, keep the soak water
- Sea salt
- Cracked pepper if you wish, to taste

OPTIONS AND VARIATIONS

1. Add 1 tsp of caraway seeds
2. Blend all ingredients except for optional caraway seeds, for 20 seconds. Add seeds & pulse through without pulverizing them.

Balsamic Maple Vinaigrette

Prep time: 5 minutes | Cook time: none | Serves 4

- 3 tbsp balsamic vinegar
- 2 tbsp maple syrup
- 1/3 cup extra-virgin olive oil
- 1 clove garlic, minced
- 1/4 tsp Dijon mustard
- Salt and pepper to taste

1. In a bowl, whisk together balsamic vinegar, maple syrup, minced garlic, Dijon mustard, salt, and pepper.
2. Slowly drizzle in the olive oil while whisking continuously until the dressing is well combined and slightly thickened.

Herb Vinaigrette

Prep time: 5 minutes | Cook time: none | Serves 4

- 1 cup high-quality extra-virgin olive oil
- 2 or 3 tablespoons white wine vinegar, rice vinegar, or sherry vinegar
- ¼ cup loosely packed fresh parsley leaves, minced
- ¼ cup loosely packed fresh oregano leaves, minced
- Pinch freshly ground black pepper

1. Add the ingredients to a small bowl, Mason jar, or salad dressing shaker.
2. Whisk to combine, or shake the bottle. Give it a shake before dressing a salad with it.

Dijon & Tarragon Dressing

Prep time: 10 minutes | Cook time: none | Serves 4

- 2 tbsp fresh tarragon leaves, chopped small (or 2 tsp dried herb)
- 1 clove garlic, minced
- 1/3 cup oil (olive or walnut or hazelnut work well)
- 2 tsp Dijon mustard
- Zest of a lemon (about a tsp)
- 1-2 tbsp lemon juice

1. Because this dressing has the sour or acid taste of the mustard. Add 1 tablespoon first and then when you're close to the desired outcome, add 1 teaspoon at a time.
2. Blend this dressing. make sure the garlic and tarragon are finely minced.

Creamy Avocado Lime Dressing

Prep time: 5 minutes | Cook time: none | Serves 4

- 1 ripe avocado, peeled and pitted
- 1/4 cup plain Greek yogurt
- 2 tbsp fresh lime juice
- 2 tbsp chopped cilantro
- 1 clove garlic, minced
- 1/4 cup olive oil
- Salt and pepper to taste

1. In a blender or food processor, combine the avocado, Greek yogurt, lime juice, cilantro, and minced garlic.
2. Blend until smooth, gradually adding olive oil while the blender is running.
3. Season with salt and pepper to taste.

Salad Renaissance

Raw Zucchini Hummus

Prep time: 10 minutes | Cook time: none | Serves 4

- 1 zucchini, chopped
- Garlic to taste (1-2 small cloves)
- 1/4 cup lemon juice
- 1/2 cup raw tahini
- 2 tbsp olive oil
- Optionally add a couple of tablespoons of raw sesame seeds

1. Simply blend this until smooth!

GARNISH

2. Remember that you can garnish with herbs, a splash of oil any seeds or decorative and tasty addition.
3. Optional: Add cayenne pepper
4. Optionally add a couple of tablespoons of raw sesame seeds

Greek Yogurt Ranch Dressing

Prep time: 5 minutes | Cook time: none | Serves 4

- 1/2 cup Greek yogurt
- 2 tbsp mayonnaise
- 1 clove garlic, minced
- 1 tbsp chopped fresh dill
- 1 tbsp chopped fresh chives
- 1 tsp onion powder
- 1 tsp Dijon mustard
- Salt and pepper to taste

1. In a bowl, whisk together Greek yogurt, mayonnaise, minced garlic, fresh dill, fresh chives, onion powder, Dijon mustard, salt, and pepper.
2. Whisk until the dressing is smooth and well combined. Adjust seasoning to taste.

Lemon Vinaigrette

Prep time: 5 minutes | Cook time: none | Serves 4

- 1 cup high-quality extra-virgin olive oil
- Grated zest of ½ lemon
- Juice of ½ lemon (about 1 to 1½ tablespoons juice)
- 1 to 1½ tablespoons white wine vinegar, rice vinegar, or sherry vinegar
- Pinch salt
- Pinch freshly ground black pepper

1. Add the ingredients to a small bowl, Mason jar, or salad dressing shaker.
2. Whisk to combine, or shake the bottle. This dressing will last up to 2 weeks at room temperature. Give it a shake before dressing a salad with it.

Ginger-Miso Vinaigrette

Prep time: 5 minutes | Cook time: none | Serves 4

- 1 large garlic clove
- ¾ cup grapeseed, vegetable, or canola oil
- ¼ cup sesame oil
- 2 tablespoons miso paste
- 1 (1-inch) piece fresh ginger, grated
- Pinch freshly ground black pepper

1. with the heel of your hand or the flat side of a knife, Slice the crushed clove.
2. Add the garlic to a small bowl, Mason jar, or salad dressing shaker along with the grapeseed oil, sesame oil, miso paste, ginger, honey, salt, and pepper. Whisk to combine. Seal the container and refrigerate for up to 4 days.

Salad Renaissance

Caesar-Style Dressing

Prep time: 5 minutes | Cook time: none | Serves 3

- 3 tablespoons vegan mayonnaise
- 1 tablespoon Dijon mustard
- 1 teaspoon red wine vinegar
- 4 teaspoons minced garlic (about 4 cloves)
- ¾ cup extra-virgin olive oil
- ¼ cup nutritional yeast
- ¼ teaspoon salt
- ¼ teaspoon freshly ground black pepper

1. In a blender or food processor, combine the mayonnaise, Worcestershire, mustard, vinegar, and garlic. Blend until the ingredients are well combined. You might need to stop and scrape down the sides during this process to ensure all ingredients are mixed well.
2. With the blender running, slowly add the olive oil until the dressing begins to thicken. Continue to add olive oil until desired consistency.
3. Transfer to a wide-mouth pint jar and close tightly with a lid.

Roasted Garlic Dressing

Prep time: 10 minutes | Cook time: 15 minutes | Makes 1 cup

- 1 head garlic
- ½ cup water
- 1 tablespoon freshly squeezed lemon juice
- 1 tablespoon maple syrup

1. Preheat the oven to 400°F.
2. Remove the outermost paper-like covering from the head of garlic while still leaving the bulbs intact to the base. Slice the top of the head of garlic so that the flesh inside the bulbs is just showing.
3. Double-wrap the head of garlic in parchment paper and place it on a baking sheet. Bake for 30 minutes.
4. In a blender, combine the caramelized garlic cloves, water, vinegar, lemon juice, and maple syrup. Blend on high for 1 minute, or until the dressing has a creamy consistency.
5. Use right away, or store in a refrigerator-safe container for up to 5 days.

Chapter 3

Vibrant Vegetable Salads and Slaws

Horiatiki Greek Country Salad

Prep time: 15 minutes | Cook time: none | Serves 4

- 1 lb. tomatoes, diced
- 1 cucumber, thinly sliced
- 1 green bell pepper, seeds removed and thinly sliced
- 1 red onion, thinly sliced
- 1/4 cup black olives
- 4 tablespoons olive oil
- 1 teaspoon sea salt
- 1/2 teaspoon oregano
- 5 ounces feta cheese
- Coarsely chopped fresh parsley for garnish

1. Arrange the vegetables in a salad bowl. Add olives and drizzle with olive oil.
2. Season with salt and oregano. Scatter feta cheese on top and sprinkle parsley.

Sweet Sesame Edamame Slaw

Prep time: 10 minutes | Cook time: none | Serves 4

- 1 (12-ounce) bag frozen edamame, thawed
- 2 cups shredded slaw mix
- 1 cup thinly sliced bell pepper
- 6 radishes, quartered
- Sweet Sesame Dressing
- ¼ cup vegetable oil
- 1 tablespoon soy sauce
- 1 tablespoon freshly squeezed lime juice
- 1 tablespoon sesame seeds

1. In a small bowl, whisk all the ingredients together. Store any leftover dressing in an airtight container in the refrigerator for up to 1 week.
2. In a large bowl, toss all the ingredients Sesame Dressing. Taste and add more dressing, if desired.

Russian Potato Salad

Prep time: 25 minutes | Cook time: 5 minutes | Serves 2

- 2 large potatoes, peeled
- 4 large carrots, peeled
- 4 eggs
- 1 (15-ounce) can sweet green peas, drained
- 4 large Mediterranean pickles
- Salt
- Freshly ground black pepper
- Pinch paprika
- ¼ cup mayonnaise

1. Bring a large pot of salted water to a boil. Add the potatoes and carrots and boil for about 15 minutes with cold water to stop the cooking process.
2. While the potatoes and carrots are cooking. Peel, dice, and place them in a large bowl.
3. Add the peas and pickles to the bowl.
4. Cut the potatoes and carrots into bite-size pieces and add to the bowl. Add the mayonnaise and mix until well combined. Serve cold.

Potato and Broccoli Salad

Prep time: 30 minutes | Cook time: none | Serves 4

- 4 potatoes, peeled
- 1 head of broccoli, broken into florets
- 1/4 cup extra-virgin olive oil
- 1/4 cup lemon juice
- 2 cloves garlic, minced
- 1 teaspoon sea salt
- 1 teaspoon cumin
- 1/4 teaspoon liquid hot pepper sauce
- 1/2 cup leeks, sliced
- 1 handful fresh parsley for garnish

1. Cook potatoes and broccoli until the vegetables are tender. Reserve and keep hot.
2. Combine the rest of ingredients in a large saucepan. Bring to a boil, stirring occasionally.
3. Pour this mixture over the vegetables. Toss to combine. Sprinkle with fresh parsley and serve.

Fiesta Chili-Lime Mixed Greens Avocado Salad

Prep time: 10 minutes | Cook time: none | Serves 4

- 1 (10-ounce) bag mixed greens
- 2 avocados, diced
- 1 cup diced English cucumber
- ¼ cup thinly sliced red onion
- Chili-Lime Vinaigrette
- ¼ cup extra-virgin olive oil
- 2 tablespoons freshly squeezed lime juice
- 1 teaspoon red pepper flakes
- ½ teaspoon dried oregano
- ½ teaspoon kosher salt
- ¼ teaspoon ground cayenne pepper
- ¼ teaspoon paprika
- ¼ teaspoon ground cumin

1. In a small bowl, whisk all the ingredients together. Taste for seasoning. Store any leftover dressing in an airtight container in the refrigerator for up to 1 week.
2. In a large bowl, toss all the ingredients together with 2 tablespoons of Chili-Lime Vinaigrette. Taste and add more dressing, if desired.

Spinach and Almonds Salad

Prep time: 15 minutes | Cook time: none | Serves 8

- 8 cups fresh spinach, torn into bite-sized pieces
- 1/2 cup slivered almonds, toasted and coarsely chopped
- 2 tablespoons sesame seeds
- 1/4 cup carrots, shredded
- 1 teaspoon salt
- 1/4 teaspoon black pepper
- 1/4 teaspoon red pepper
- 1/2 teaspoon basil
- 1 teaspoon onion powder
- Juice of 1 fresh lime
- 2 tablespoons olive oil
- 2 cloves garlic, minced

1. In a large mixing bowl, combine spinach, almonds, sesame seeds and carrots. Toss to combine well.
2. To make the dressing: In a separate bowl, whisk salt, spices, lime juice, olive oil and garlic.
3. Drizzle prepared dressing over spinach mixture in the large bowl. Serve at room temperature or chilled.

Salad Renaissance

Waldorf Salad

Prep time: 5 minutes | Cook time: none | Serves 4

Salad

- 1 stalk celery finely sliced
- 2 apples diced
- 1/2 cup walnuts, chopped
- 1/2 small onion diced
- 1/2 medium red bell pepper (capsicum) diced or sliced
- Optional: A lovely touch is adding 1/2 cup dried raisins (or sultanas)
- Optional: Some halved seedless grapes

1. Combine the salad, add a dressing and gently toss.

DRESSING RECOMMENDATIONS

2. The classic thing with a Waldorf Salad is to dress it with a creamy dressing.

Italian Sub Salad

Prep time: 10 minutes | Cook time: none | Serves 4

- 1 (10-ounce) bag chopped Romaine lettuce
- 2 Roma tomatoes, chopped
- 1½ cups shredded mozzarella
- ½ red onion, thinly sliced
- ½ cup giardiniera
- Italian Dressing
- ¼ cup extra-virgin olive oil
- 2 tablespoons red wine vinegar
- 1 tablespoon dried Italian seasoning
- 1 teaspoon Dijon mustard
- ½ teaspoon red pepper flakes

1. In a small bowl, whisk all the ingredients together.dressing in an airtight container in the refrigerator for up to 1 week.
2. In a large bowl, gently toss the lettuce, tomatoes, bell pepper, mozzarella, Taste and add more dressing, if desired.

Bountiful Seaweed Salad

Prep time: 10 minutes | Cook time: none | Serves 4

- 2 cups seaweed
- 1/2 cup cucumber, julienned
- 1 cup red pepper in matchsticks
- 1/2 small onion, finely sliced
- 2 cups of green leafy vegetables
- 1 cup of green papaya, spiral or julienne grated
- 1 medium carrot, peeled, cut in matchsticks
- 1/2 beet, peeled, cut in matchsticks
- Optional: 1-2 small red chilli peppers, deseeded, minced

1. Prepare the green papaya and squirt with a little Bragg Liquid Aminos before adding to the rest of the salad. You can use tamari, soy sauce or coconut aminos.
2. Combine all ingredients except your garnishes. Top with your sesame seeds.

Detox Red Cabbage Kale Slaw

Prep time: 10 minutes | Cook time: none | Serves 4

- 1 (10-ounce) package shredded red cabbage
- 1 (10-ounce) package baby kale
- ¼ cup toasted pumpkin seeds
- ¼ cup dried cranberries
- Cranberry Honey Vinaigrette
- ¼ cup extra-virgin olive oil
- 2 tablespoons cranberry juice
- 2 teaspoons honey
- Freshly ground black pepper

1. In a small bowl, whisk all the ingredients together until the salt has dissolved. dressing in an airtight container in the refrigerator for up to 1 week.
2. In a large bowl, toss all the ingredients Vinaigrette. Taste and add more dressing, if desired.

20 | *Salad Renaissance*

Cucumber and Onion Quinoa Salad

Prep time: 15 minutes | Cook time: 20 minutes | Serves 4

- 1½ cups dry quinoa, rinsed and drained
- 2¼ cups water
- ⅓ cup white wine vinegar
- 2 tablespoons extra-virgin olive oil
- 1 tablespoon chopped fresh dill
- 1½ teaspoons vegan sugar
- 2 pinches salt
- 2 cups diced cucumber
- 4 cups shredded lettuce

1. In a medium pot, combine the quinoa and water. Bring to a boil. Cover, reduce the heat to medium-low, and simmer for 15 to 20 minutes, until the water is absorbed.
2. Remove from the stove and let stand for 5 minutes.
3. Fluff with a fork and set aside.
4. Into each of 4 wide-mouth jars, add Seal the lids tightly.

Caramelized Onion and Beet Salad

Prep time: 10 minutes | Cook time: 40 minutes | Serves 4

- 3 medium golden beets
- 2 cups sliced sweet or Vidalia onions
- 1 teaspoon extra-virgin olive oil or no-beef broth
- Pinch baking soda
- ¼ to ½ teaspoon salt, to taste
- 2 tablespoons unseasoned rice vinegar, white wine vinegar, or balsamic vinegar

1. Cut the greens off the beets, and scrub the beets. In a large pot, place a until you can easily pierce the middle of the beets with a knife.
2. Meanwhile, in a large, dry skillet over medium heat, sauté the onions for 5 minutes, stirring frequently. Transfer to a large bowl and set aside.
3. Divide the beets evenly among 4 wide-mouth jars or storage containers. Let cool before sealing the lids.

Chapter 4

Wholesome Grain, Bean, and Pasta Salads

Italian Bean and Rice Salad

Prep time: 25 minutes | Cook time: none | Serves 6

- 2 cups cooked long-grain rice
- 1 cup cooked beans
- 1 cup cherry tomatoes, halved
- 2 ounces Cheddar cheese, shredded
- 1/4 cup Italian dressing
- 1 tablespoon balsamic vinegar
- 1 tablespoon lemon zest
- Sea salt to taste
- Black pepper to taste
- Lettuce leaves for garnish

1. Combine rice, beans, tomatoes, and cheese in a large bowl. Toss to combine.
2. Pour Italian dressing and vinegar over the mixture in the bowl.
3. Toss again and sprinkle lemon zest. Season with salt and pepper to taste and adjust the seasonings. Serve on lettuce leaves.

Farro Grape Salad

Prep time: 10 minutes | Cook time: 20 minutes | Serves 4

- 2 cups water
- 1 cup uncooked pearl farro
- 1 cup halved seedless grapes
- ½ cup chopped pecans
- Grape Balsamic Dressing
- 2 tablespoons balsamic vinegar
- 1 tablespoon grape jelly
- 2 teaspoons Dijon mustard
- Freshly ground black pepper

1. In a small bowl, whisk all the ingredients together.dressing in an airtight container in the refrigerator for up to 1 week.
2. In a saucepan, bring the water to a boil and add the farro. Drain any excess water and cool.
3. In a large bowl, toss the farro, spinach, grapes, and pecans with 3 tablespoons Taste and add more dressing, if desired.
4. Top with feta cheese and serve.

Salad Renaissance | 23

Spiced Lentil Salad

Prep time: 30 minutes | Cook time: 20 minutes | Serves 8

- 1 cup brown lentils
- 1 cup carrots, thinly sliced
- 1 cup green onion, finely chopped
- 2 cloves garlic, minced
- 1/2 teaspoon dried thyme
- 1/4 cup olive oil
- 1 teaspoon salt
- 1/4 teaspoon ground black pepper
- 1/4 teaspoon paprika

1. In a large saucepan, over medium-high heat, combine lentils, carrots, green onion, garlic and thyme.
2. Add enough water to cover and bring to boil. simmer for 15 to 20 minutes.
3. Drain lentils and vegetables. Add olive oil, lemon juice, celery, parsley, salt, black pepper and paprika. Toss to mix ingredients and serve at room temperature.

Mexican Pasta Salad

Prep time: 20 minutes | Cook time: 5 minutes | Serves 3 or 4

- 8 ounces rotini pasta
- 1 (15-ounce) can kidney beans, drained and rinsed
- 4 scallions, green parts only, thinly sliced
- ½ cup pepitas or sunflower seeds
- ¾ cup crumbled cotija cheese
- 6 tablespoons Avocado-Yogurt Dressing
- Salt
- Freshly ground black pepper

1. Cook the rotini according to the package instructions. Drain the pasta and run it under cold water. Place in a medium bowl.
2. Add the beans, scallion greens, pepitas, cotija, and dressing. Season with salt and pepper and toss to combine.
3. Divide the salad between three or four bowls. Serve at room temperature.

Corn Bread and Bacon Salad

Prep time: 15 minutes | Cook time: none | Serves 12

- 1 loaf corn bread
- 8 slices cooked bacon, crumbled
- 1/2 cup leeks, chopped
- 2 large tomatoes, diced
- 2 hard-boiled eggs, thinly sliced
- 1 cup mayonnaise
- 1/2 teaspoon cumin seeds
- 1/2 teaspoon salt
- 1/2 teaspoon red pepper flakes

1. Cut corn bread into bite-sized cubes. Transfer the bread cubes to a large salad bowl and add bacon, leeks, tomatoes, and eggs. Stir to combine.
2. Add mayonnaise, cumin seeds and salt. Gently stir to combine. Taste and adjust the seasonings.
3. Sprinkle red pepper flakes on the top end serve very chilled.

Kale Pesto Pasta Salad

Prep time: 30 minutes | Cook time: 5 minutes | Serves 3

- 3 cups fresh kale
- 3 tablespoons walnuts
- ½ cup grated Parmesan cheese, plus more for garnish
- Salt
- Freshly ground black pepper
- 6 ounces whole-wheat rotini or other pasta

1. To make the pesto, place the kale in the bowl of a food processor or in a blender. add more lemon juice or oil. This yields a little less than 1 cup of pesto.
2. Cook the pasta. Reserve 1 tablespoon of the starchy pasta cooking water.
3. Heat the remaining 2 tablespoons of olive oil in a large skillet over medium heat. Add the pasta and stir to combine.
4. Divide the pasta salad between three bowls. Serve warm, garnished with freshly grated Parmesan cheese.

Salad Renaissance

Curried Pasta Salad

Prep time: 40 minutes | Cook time: none | Serves 4

- 1/4 cup olive oil
- 2 tablespoons wine vinegar
- 2 tablespoons chives, minced
- 1 teaspoon dry mustard
- 1/4 teaspoon black pepper
- 1 pound lean pork, cooked
- 1 cup macaroni
- 1 cucumbers, peeled, seeded and julienned
- 1 teaspoon salt
- 1/4 cup mayonnaise
- 1 tablespoon curry powder

1. To make the dressing: Combine olive oil, vinegar, chives, mustard and black pepper. Marinate the pork in this dressing for 1 hour.
2. Cook macaroni al dente. Drain, cool and reserve.
3. Combine cucumber with salt and reserve in a salad bowl. Rinse, drain and pat dry. Add pork, macaroni, mayonnaise, and curry powder to the salad bowl. Toss and serve chilled.

Tomato-Ramen Salad

Prep time: 30 minutes | Cook time: 5 minutes | Serves 4

- 1 (8-ounce) package rice noodles
- 4 tablespoons sesame, grapeseed, canola, or vegetable oil, divided
- 12 ounces firm tofu, cubed
- 2 cups cherry tomatoes, halved
- 4 large scallions, greens parts only
- 4 eggs
- ½ cup Ginger-Miso Vinaigrette

1. Preheat the broiler.
2. Prepare the rice noodles according to the instructions on the package.
3. Heat 2 tablespoons of oil in a large skillet over medium-high heat.pan-fry them until golden brown on all sides, 1 to 2 minutes per side.
4. Roughly chop the broiled scallion greens.
5. While the tomatoes and scallions are roasting, soft-boil the eggs. Once chilled, peel the eggs.
6. Divide the rice noodles, tofu, tomatoes, and chopped scallions among four bowls. Serve warm.

Greek Pasta Salad

Prep time: 35 minutes | Cook time: none | Serves 4

- 12 ounces fusilli pasta
- 1 cucumber, thinly sliced
- 2 tomatoes, diced
- 2 roasted red bell peppers, sliced
- 1/2 cup leeks, sliced
- 1 teaspoon garlic powder
- 1/4 cup olives, pitted
- 1/2 dried basil
- 1/2 dried oregano
- 1 cup feta cheese, crumbled
- 1/2 cup salad dressing

1. Cook fusilli pasta according to the directions on the package.
2. Drain the pasta and rinse under the cold, running water.
3. Combine together cucumber, tomatoes, red bell pepper, leeks, garlic, olives, basil and oregano.
4. Add cooked pasta and toss to combine. Pour in dressing, scatter feta cheese on top and serve.

Green Brown Rice Salad

Prep time: 10 minutes | Cook time: 5 minutes | Serves 4

- 1 (8-ounce) box instant brown rice
- 1 (8-ounce) bag fresh spinach, roughly chopped
- ½ cup diced zucchini
- ¼ cup chopped scallions, green part only
- ¼ cup chopped fresh parsley
- ¼ cup crumbled feta
- 1 garlic clove, minced
- 1 teaspoon granulated sugar
- 1 teaspoon Dijon mustard
- ½ teaspoon red pepper flakes

1. In a small bowl, whisk all the ingredients together until the sugar has dissolved. Taste for seasoning. Store any leftover dressing in an airtight container in the refrigerator for up to 1 week.
2. Cook the brown rice according to package instructions and set aside to cool.
3. In a large bowl, toss together the spinach, zucchini, scallions, parsley, and feta Taste and add more dressing, if desired.

Garden Pasta Salad

Prep time: 30 minutes | Cook time: 2 hours | Serves 8 to 10

- 4 quarts water
- one 10- to 12-ounce package tricolor rotini pasta
- 1 cup chopped broccoli
- 1 cup chopped cauliflower
- 1 cup sliced mushrooms
- 3 scallions, thinly sliced
- one 2-ounce jar chopped pimientos, drained
- freshly ground black pepper to taste

1. Bring the water to a boil and add the pasta. Return to boiling and cook, uncovered, for 6 minutes. Drain. Rinse under cool water and set aside.
2. Place the broccoli, cauliflower, and snow peas in a steamer basket. Steam over boiling water for 4 to 5 minutes, until tender-crisp.
3. Combine all of the ingredients in a large bowl. Toss to mix well. Refrigerate for at least 2 hours before serving.

Buffalo Chickpea Salad

Prep time: 10 minutes | Cook time: 10 minutes | Makes 2 salads

- Sweet Hummus Dressing:
- ¼ cup pumpkin hummus or other hummus
- 2 teaspoons 100% maple syrup
- 2 tablespoons red wine vinegar or freshly squeezed lemon juice
- 2 teaspoons hot water
- Buffalo Chickpeas:
- 2 teaspoons garlic-infused olive oil
- ¼ cup halved cherry tomatoes

4. Make the dressing: Whisk together the hummus, maple syrup, and vinegar until creamy and smooth. Keep whisking while slowly adding in the hot water. The dressing should be thick but pourable. Add more water as needed.
5. Make the salad: Toss the romaine with the dressing, then gently toss in the avocado, tomatoes, and buffalo chickpeas. Divide between two bowls and serve immediately.

The Daily Salad

Prep time: 10 minutes | Cook time: 10 minutes | Serves 2

- 4 cups chopped leafy greens
- ½ cup quick-pickled beets (recipe follows), or store-bought
- ½ cup cooked chickpeas
- ¼ cup sunflower seeds
- handful broccoli sprouts
- 1 medium carrot, shredded
- 10 cherry tomatoes, sliced
- Oil-Free Orange Dressing:
- Supercharged Roasted Roots (optional; recipe follows), for serving

1. Make the salad: In a large bowl, toss together the greens, pickled beets, chickpeas, sunflower seeds, sprouts, carrots, tomatoes, and any other Supercharge toppings, if using. Set aside.
2. When ready to serve, drizzle each salad with ¼ cup dressing, toss well, and add salt and pepper to taste.

Mediterranean Grain Salad

Prep time: 10 minutes | Cook time: 10 minutes | Makes 6 cups

- Mediterranean Grain Salad:
- 1 cup uncooked farro
- 1 cup chickpeas
- 1 large tomato, diced
- 1 medium red bell pepper, chopped
- 1 medium yellow bell pepper, chopped
- salt and freshly ground black pepper
- 3 tablespoons olive oil

1. Make the grain salad: Bring 3 cups Drain and rinse under cold water and set aside.
2. Combine the cooked farro, chickpeas, tomato, red and yellow bell peppers, cucumber, olives, and parsley in a large bowl and toss together. Set aside.
3. Assemble: Toss the dressing with the grain salad until well combined, adding more salt and pepper as desired. Store in the fridge. Leftovers will keep for 2 to 3 days in the fridge.

Salad Renaissance

Chapter 5

Tasty Tofu and Egg Salads

Vegan Smoked Tofu Salad

Prep time: 15 minutes | Cook time: none | Serves 6

- 16 ounces smoked tofu
- 1 cup grapes
- 1 cup slivered almonds
- 1 cup scallions
- 2 carrots, thinly sliced
- 1 recipe Orange Poppy Seed Dressing
- 1/2 teaspoon salt
- 1/4 teaspoon black pepper
- 1/2 teaspoon celery seeds
- Baby spinach for garnish

1. Cut the tofu into bite-sized cubes. In a large salad bowl, combine tofu with the grapes, almonds, scallions, carrots, dressing, and salt, pepper and celery seeds.
2. Serve on a bed of baby spinach.

Summer Cucumber Egg Salad

Prep time: 15 minutes | Cook time: none | Serves 2

- 1 cucumber, thinly sliced
- 1 cup fresh cilantro, chopped
- 2 tablespoons rice vinegar
- 1 teaspoon sea salt
- 2 hard-boiled eggs, quartered
- 1/2 teaspoon fresh dill

1. In a medium bowl, mix cucumber, cilantro, vinegar, and salt together. Stir to combine.
2. Garnish with eggs and sprinkle fresh dill on top.
3. Taste, adjust the seasonings and serve at room temperature or chilled.

Cold Carrot Tofu Salad

Prep time: 10 minutes | Cook time: none | Serves 4

- 1 (12-ounce) package firm tofu, drained and cut into 1-inch cubes
- 1 (8-ounce) bag shredded carrots
- Thai Chili Soy Dressing
- ¼ cup vegetable oil
- 2 scallions, green part only, finely chopped
- 2 tablespoons soy sauce
- 2 tablespoons rice wine vinegar
- 2 to 3 Thai chilis, chopped
- 1 garlic clove, minced

1. In a small bowl, whisk all the ingredients together. Taste for seasoning. Store any leftover dressing in an airtight container in the refrigerator for up to 1 week.
2. In a large bowl, toss the tofu, carrots, and all of the Thai Chili Soy Dressing together. Marinate for at least 10 minutes before serving.

Chilled Miso Tofu, Cucumber, and Radish Salad

Prep time: 30 minutes | Cook time: 5 minutes | Serves 3

- 3 large carrots
- 1 tablespoon rice vinegar
- 2 Persian cucumbers
- 2 large radishes
- 1 pound firm tofu
- 6 cups mizuna greens
- 6 tablespoons Ginger-Miso Vinaigrette

1. Use a vegetable peeler to shave the carrots into ribbons. Place them in a large bowl and toss them with the vinegar.
2. Halve the radishes, then slice into half-moons as thinly as possible.toss to combine.
3. Cube the tofu and add it to the vegetables.
4. Add the mizuna greens to the bowl. Drizzle with the vinaigrette and toss to combine.
5. Refrigerate the salad for at least 15 minutes before serving. Serve cold.

BBQ Tofu and Quinoa Salad

Prep time: 20 minutes | Cook time: 20 minutes | Serves 4

- 14 oz extra-firm tofu, pressed and cut into cubes
- 1 cup quinoa, cooked
- 1 cup cherry tomatoes, halved
- 1/2 red onion, finely chopped
- 1/4 cup fresh cilantro, chopped
- 2 tbsp olive oil
- 2 tbsp BBQ sauce
- 1 tbsp apple cider vinegar
- 1 tsp smoked paprika
- Salt and pepper to taste

1. Preheat the oven to 400°F.
2. Toss tofu cubes with olive oil, BBQ sauce, apple cider vinegar, smoked paprika, salt, and pepper.
3. In a large bowl, combine cooked quinoa, cherry tomatoes, diced cucumber, finely chopped red onion, and fresh cilantro.
4. Add the BBQ tofu to the salad and gently toss.
5. Serve the salad warm or chilled, adjusting the seasoning if needed.

Teriyaki Snow Pea Tofu Salad

Prep time: 10 minutes | Cook time: 13 minutes | Serves 4

- 1 (12-ounce) package extra-firm tofu, drained
- 2 tablespoons vegetable oil
- ¼ cup teriyaki sauce
- 2 cups snow peas
- 1 cup zucchini, cut into half-moons
- ¼ cup peanut butter
- 1 tablespoon soy sauce
- 1 teaspoon ground ginger
- ½ teaspoon garlic powder

1. In a small bowl, whisk all the ingredients together. Taste for seasoning. Store any leftover dressing in an airtight container in the refrigerator for up to 1 week.
2. Place the tofu between paper towels and Place a weight on the tofu and let sit for 5 minutes. Cut into ½-inch-thick strips.
3. Top with walnuts and feta. Drizzle with 3 tablespoons of Peanut Dressing. Taste and add more dressing, if desired.

Salad Renaissance

Classic Egg Salad

Prep time: 15 minutes | Cook time: 12 minutes | Serves 4

- 6 hard-boiled eggs, peeled and chopped
- 1/4 cup mayonnaise
- 1 teaspoon Dijon mustard
- 1/2 teaspoon white vinegar
- Salt and pepper to taste
- 2 tablespoons finely chopped celery
- Chopped fresh parsley for garnish (optional)

1. In a bowl, combine chopped eggs, mayonnaise, Dijon mustard, vinegar, salt, and pepper. Mix well.
2. Add celery and red onion, if using. Stir until evenly distributed.
3. Taste and adjust seasoning if needed.
4. Garnish with chopped parsley.
5. Serve as a sandwich, on crackers, or over a bed of lettuce.

Avocado Egg Salad

Prep time: 15 minutes | Cook time: 12 minutes | Serves 4

- 6 hard-boiled eggs, chopped
- 2 ripe avocados, diced
- 1/4 cup red onion, finely chopped
- 2 tablespoons fresh cilantro, chopped
- Juice of 1 lime
- Salt and pepper to taste
- Optional: Hot sauce for a kick

1. In a bowl, combine chopped hard-boiled eggs, diced avocados, chopped red onion, and cilantro.
2. Squeeze lime juice over the mixture and gently toss to combine.
3. Season with salt and pepper. Add hot sauce if you like it spicy.
4. Serve on toast, crackers, or in a sandwich. Enjoy this creamy avocado twist on classic egg salad!

Mashed Potato Salad with Eggs

Prep time: 30 minutes | Cook time: none | Serves 4

- 2 lbs. new potatoes, chopped
- 1 large onion, finely chopped
- 3 hard-boiled eggs, chopped
- 2 cloves garlic, minced
- 1/2 cup mayonnaise
- Tabasco sauce to taste
- Juice of 1 fresh lemon
- 1/4 teaspoon black pepper

1. Place the potatoes in a large stockpot and cover with salted water. Reduce the heat and cook until the potatoes are fork tender.
2. Drain the potatoes and transfer them to a large bowl. Mash the potatoes.
3. Then, stir in the onions, eggs, garlic, mayonnaise, and yellow mustard. Add Tabasco sauce and lemon juice. Season with salt and black pepper. Serve chilled.

Sesame Ginger Tofu Salad

Prep time: 15 minutes | Cook time: 15 minutes | Serves 4

- 14 oz firm tofu, pressed and cubed
- 4 cups mixed salad greens
- 1 carrot, julienned
- 2 green onions, sliced
- 2 tbsp sesame oil
- 2 tbsp soy sauce
- 1 clove garlic, minced
- 1 tsp maple syrup
- 1 tbsp sesame seeds (for garnish)

1. In a pan, heat sesame oil over medium heat. Add cubed tofu and cook until golden brown on all sides.
2. In a large salad bowl, combine mixed greens, shredded red cabbage, julienned carrot, and sliced green onions.
3. Add the cooked tofu to the salad and drizzle the dressing over the top.
4. Toss the salad gently to combine all ingredients. Sprinkle sesame seeds on top for garnish.

Salad Renaissance

Creamy Potato and Tofu Salad

Prep time: 10 minutes | **Cook time:** 20 minutes | **Serves 4**

- 5 large red or golden potatoes, cut into 1-inch cubes
- 1 cup silken tofu or 1 large avocado
- ¼ cup chopped fresh chives
- ½ teaspoon garlic powder
- ½ teaspoon onion powder
- ½ teaspoon dried dill
- ¼ teaspoon freshly ground black pepper

1. Bring a large pot of water to a boil over high heat. Immerse the potatoes in the hot water gently and carefully. Boil for 10 minutes, or until the potatoes can be easily pierced with a fork. Drain.
2. Put the potatoes in a large bowl, and refrigerate for a minimum of 20 minutes.

Tofu "Egg" Salad

Prep time: 10 minutes | **Cook time:** 1 hour | **Makes 2 cups**

- 1 pound firm tofu, drained and crumbled
- ¼ cup fat-free mayonnaise (optional)
- 2 tablespoons prepared mustard
- 1 tablespoon soy sauce
- ½ teaspoon ground turmeric
- 3 to 4 scallions, finely chopped
- ¼ cup minced celery
- ⅛ cup pickle relish (optional)

1. Place the tofu in a bowl and mash with a potato masher. Add the mayonnaise (if desired), mustard, soy sauce, and turmeric. Mix well until the tofu takes on a bright yellow color.
2. Stir in the scallions, celery, and relish, if desired. Chill 1 hour or more before serving.

Hearty Chopped Salad

Prep time: 15 minutes | Cook time: 25 minutes | Serves 2

- 4 slices whole30-compliant bacon
- 4 cups chopped romaine lettuce
- 1 small unpeeled cucumber, chopped
- 1 cup grape tomatoes, halved
- whole30-compliant ranch salad dressing or whole30 ranch dressing
- ¼ teaspoon salt
- ¼ teaspoon black pepper

1. Cook the bacon in a large skillet over medium heat until crisp, about 10 minutes. Remove with a slotted spoon and place on paper towels to drain. Crumble the bacon when cool enough to handle.
2. Arrange the lettuce on two plates. Top with the chicken, bacon, eggs, Toss to combine and serve.

Bistro Breakfast Salad

Prep time: 10 minutes | Cook time: 30 minutes | Serves 2

- 4 cups packed curly endive
- 1½ tablespoons extra-virgin olive oil
- 1 tablespoon apple cider vinegar
- 1 teaspoon whole30-compliant dijon mustard
- ¼ teaspoon minced garlic
- salt and black pepper
- 4 slices whole30-compliant bacon, cut into ¼-inch pieces
- 2 teaspoons white vinegar
- 4 large eggs

1. Wash and dry the endive. Place in a shallow salad bowl and chill until needed.
2. Combine the oil, apple cider vinegar, mustard, and garlic in a small jar with a lid. Season with salt and pepper. Cover and shake vigorously to combine. Set aside.

Salad Renaissance | 37

Chapter 6

Fresh Fish and Seafood Salads

Shrimp and Peas Pasta Salad

Prep time: 25 minutes | Cook time: none | Serves 4

- 1 cup pasta of choice
- 1/3 cup leeks, chopped
- 1 cup frozen peas
- 6 ounces baby shrimp
- 1 carrot, grated
- 1 cup plain yogurt
- 3 tablespoons low-fat mayonnaise
- 1 teaspoon Dijon mustard
- 1 teaspoon garlic salt
- 1/2 teaspoon garlic pepper
- 1 teaspoon celery seeds

1. Cook your favorite pasta until al dente or for 12 to 15 minutes. Drain and rinse pasta.
2. Mix chilled pasta with the rest of ingredients. Mix well to combine.
3. Serve chilled.

Mediterranean Quinoa-Salmon Salad

Prep time: 35 minutes | Cook time: 5 minutes | Serves 2

- ¾ cup quinoa
- 2 (5-ounce) salmon fillets
- Salt
- 2 large tomatoes, finely chopped
- ½ small red onion, finely chopped
- ½ cup crumbled feta cheese
- ¼ cup Herb Vinaigrette

1. Cook the quinoa according to the instructions on the package. Once cooked, fluff the quinoa with a fork.
2. Season the salmon generously on both sides with the salt and pepper. Pan-sear it.
3. Place the quinoa, tomatoes, red onion, salmon and feta in a large bowl. Drizzle with the vinaigrette and toss to combine.
4. Divide the salad between two bowls. Serve warm or cold.

Honey Chipotle Fire Shrimp Salad

Prep time: 10 minutes | Cook time: 7 minutes | Serves 4

- 2 tablespoons extra-virgin olive oil
- 1 pound frozen shrimp, thawed, shelled and deveined
- 2 teaspoons adobo sauce, from can of chipotle peppers
- 1 cup halved cherry tomatoes
- 2 teaspoons adobo sauce, from can of chipotle peppers
- ½ teaspoon kosher salt

1. In a blender, combine all the ingredients. Store any leftover dressing in an airtight container in the refrigerator for up to 1 week.
2. Add the shrimp and sauté for about 2 minutes.
3. Add the adobo sauce and the salt. Turn off the heat.
4. In a large bowl, toss the lettuce, beans, corn, and tomatoes with 3 tablespoons of Honey Chipotle Dressing. Taste and add more dressing, if desired.

Smoked Salmon and Egg Salad

Prep time: 15 minutes | Cook time: 5 minutes | Serves 4

- 8 eggs
- 8 cups mixed greens
- ½ cup Lemon Vinaigrette
- 2 large Persian cucumbers, halved lengthwise and cut into half-moons
- 1½ tablespoons pickled red onions
- 8 ounces smoked salmon lox
- Salt
- Freshly ground black pepper

1. Soft-boil the eggs. Peel and set aside.
2. In a large bowl, toss the mixed greens with the vinaigrette. Add the cucumbers and pickled red onions and toss to combine.
3. Divide the salad among four plates. Gently pull apart the lox slices and add some to each salad. Halve the soft-boiled eggs lengthwise and top each salad with them. Season generously with salt and pepper. Serve while the eggs are warm.

Lobster and Egg Salad

Prep time: 50 minutes | Cook time: none | Serves 6

- 2 cup lobster meat
- 1 cup diced celery
- French dressing
- Mayonnaise
- 2 hard-cooked eggs
- 10-12 black olives
- Salt to taste
- Black pepper to taste

1. Combine lobster meat and celery together. Marinate this mixture with French dressing for 30 minutes. Drain off the dressing.
2. Heap the salad mixture on the salad bowl. Garnished with mayonnaise, eggs, and olives. Sprinkle with salt and pepper and serve chilled.

Lunchbox Tuna Chickpea Salad

Prep time: 10 minutes | Cook time: none | Serves 4

- 4 (5-ounce) cans water-packed tuna, drained
- 1 (15-ounce) can chickpeas, drained and rinsed
- 1 (8-ounce) bag arugula
- ¼ cup chopped scallions, green part only
- Kalamata Feta Vinaigrette
- 4 to 6 Kalamata olives, pitted
- ¼ cup extra-virgin olive oil

1. In a food processor, combine the feta, olives, lemon juice, garlic, oregano, and red pepper flakes. Scrape the sides of the bowl.
2. Store any leftover dressing in an airtight container in the refrigerator for up to 1 week.
3. In a large bowl, toss all the ingredients together with 3 tablespoons of Kalamata Feta Vinaigrette. Taste and add more dressing, if desired.

Salad Renaissance | 41

Tuna and Cannellini Bean Salad

Prep time: 5 minutes | Cook time: 5 minutes | Serves 2

- 1 (15-ounce) can cannellini beans, drained and rinsed
- 1 cup packed fresh parsley leaves, finely chopped
- 2 (4-ounce) cans chunk light tuna packed in water, drained
- 2 garlic cloves, minced
- Grated zest and juice of 1 lemon
- ¼ cup extra-virgin olive oil
- Salt
- Freshly ground black pepper

1. Combine the beans, parsley, tuna, garlic, lemon zest and juice, and olive oil in a medium bowl. Season with salt and pepper.
2. Divide the salad between two bowls. Serve cold or at room temperature.

Shrimp Cobb Salad

Prep time: 15 minutes | Cook time: 5 minutes | Serves 1

- 2 large eggs
- 2 cups torn romaine lettuce
- 4 ounces cooked shrimp, diced
- ½ cup drained canned sweet corn
- ⅓ cup crumbled feta cheese
- Salt
- Freshly ground black pepper
- 2 tablespoons Avocado-Yogurt Dressing

1. Hard-boil the eggs. Chill, peel and dice the eggs.
2. Place the romaine on a plate. Add the shrimp in a long stripe across one side of the lettuce. Do the same with the eggs, corn, and crumbled feta so that the four ingredients are right in a row. Season the salad with salt and pepper and drizzle with the dressing. Serve at room temperature.

Classic Shrimp and Avocado Salad

Prep time: 15 minutes | Cook time: 5 minutes | Serves 4

- 1 lb large shrimp, peeled and deveined
- 2 avocados, diced
- 1 cup cherry tomatoes, halved
- 1/4 cup red onion, finely chopped
- 1/4 cup fresh cilantro, chopped
- Juice of 2 limes
- 2 tbsp olive oil
- Salt and pepper to taste
- Mixed salad greens for serving

1. Bring a pot of water to a boil and cook the shrimp for 3-5 minutes until they turn pink and opaque. Drain and let them cool.
2. In a large bowl, combine diced avocados, halved cherry tomatoes, finely chopped red onion, and fresh cilantro.
3. Add the cooked shrimp to the bowl.
4. Serve the shrimp and avocado salad over a bed of mixed salad greens.

Grilled Salmon Caesar Salad

Prep time: 15 minutes | Cook time: 10 minutes | Serves 4

- 1 lb salmon fillets
- 1 tsp olive oil
- 1 tsp lemon zest
- Salt and black pepper to taste
- 1 cup cherry tomatoes, halved
- 1/2 cup grated Parmesan cheese
- 1/2 cup Caesar dressing (store-bought or homemade)

1. Preheat the grill or a grill pan over medium-high heat.
2. Brush salmon fillets with olive oil, sprinkle with lemon zest, salt, and pepper.
3. Grill the salmon for about 4-5 minutes per side or until it flakes easily with a fork.
4. Add the grilled salmon to the salad.
5. Drizzle Caesar dressing over the top and toss gently to coat.
6. Serve the grilled salmon Caesar salad immediately.

Salad Renaissance | 43

Smoked Salmon and Yam Salad

Prep time: 25 minutes | Cook time: 35 minutes | Serves 6

Salad:
- 3½ to 4 pounds yams, peeled and cubed
- ½ pound smoked salmon
- 4 to 5 green onions, sliced into rounds
- ½ cup chopped fresh cilantro

Dressing:
- ½ cup raw cashews
- 6 to 8 tablespoons water
- ¼ cup freshly squeezed lime juice
- ¾ to 1 teaspoon sea salt or Herbamare
- ¼ to ½ teaspoon chipotle chile powder

1. To make the salad, cook the cubed yams in a steamer basket over about 2 inches of water in a 2- or 3-quart pot. Transfer to a plate or platter to cool completely.
2. In a large bowl, combine the cooled yams and remaining salad ingredients and gently toss together.

Hot-And-Sour Salmon Salad

Prep time: 10 minutes | Cook time: 20 minutes | Serves 4

- 1 cup cider vinegar
- ½ cup thinly sliced radishes
- ½ cup matchstick carrots
- ½ cup thinly sliced cucumber
- ½ teaspoon salt
- 4 skinless salmon fillets (4 ounces each)
- cracked black pepper
- 2 tablespoons avocado oil
- 2 tablespoons fresh lemon juice
- 1 package (5 ounces) mixed salad greens
- 2 tablespoons chopped fresh chives

1. In a small bowl, combine the vinegar, radishes, carrots, cucumber, and ¼ teaspoon of the salt. Let sit while preparing the salmon.
2. Select Manual and cook on high pressure for 3 minutes. Use quick release. Remove the salmon.

Asian Tuna, Snow Pea, and Broccoli Salad

Prep time: 10 minutes | Cook time: 10 minutes | Serves 4

For The Dressing:
- 1 teaspoon grated orange zest
- 3 tablespoons extra-virgin olive oil
- 3 tablespoons rice vinegar
- 1 tablespoon toasted sesame oil

For The Salad:
- 1 orange, peeled and cut into bite-size pieces
- 1 bag (12 ounces) broccoli slaw
- 1 package (8 ounces) fresh snow peas, trimmed and halved diagonally
- 2 cans (5 ounces each) water-packed wild albacore tuna, drained and broken into chunks

1. Make the dressing: In a small bowl, combine the orange zest, olive oil, vinegar, and sesame oil.
2. Make the salad: In a large bowl, combine the orange pieces with the broccoli slaw, snow peas, and tuna. Drizzle with the dressing and gently toss.

Warm Salmon and Potato Salad

Prep time: 10 minutes | Cook time: 25 minutes | Serves 4

- 1½ pounds baby yellow potatoes, halved
- ⅓ cup avocado oil
- 1 tablespoon fresh lemon juice
- ½ teaspoon salt
- ½ teaspoon black pepper
- 1 can (6 ounces) salmon, drained
- 2 cups arugula
- 3 green onions, sliced
- 2 tablespoons snipped fresh chives
- 1 tablespoon minced fresh parsley

1. Place the potatoes in a medium pot and add enough cold water to cover. Bring to a low boil and cook until tender, about 15 minutes. Drain.
2. In a large bowl, whisk together the avocado oil, mustard, lemon juice, salt, and pepper. Add the potatoes, salmon, arugula, green onions, chives, and parsley. Gently toss until the potatoes are coated. Serve warm.

Chapter 7

Scrumptious Chicken Salads

Asparagus Chicken Salad

Prep time: 40 minutes | Cook time: none | Serves 4

- 1/4 cup Parmesan cheese
- 1/4 cup breadcrumbs
- 4 chicken breast halves, boneless and skinless
- 6 cups spinach leaves, stems removed
- 3 cups cooked rice
- 1 pound asparagus, blanched and cut into bite-sized pieces
- 2/3 cup Vinaigrette salad dressing
- Handful fresh parsley, roughly chopped

1. In a medium bowl, combine cheese with breadcrumbs. Coat chicken breasts with this mixture.
2. Heat olive oil in a wide saucepan over medium-high heat. Transfer the chicken to the large bowl and set aside.
3. Add spinach, rice, asparagus, tomatoes, leeks, and walnuts. Toss to combine.
4. Pour Vinaigrette salad dressing over salad just before serving and serve chilled.

Chicken Orange Salad

Prep time: 25 minutes | Cook time: none | Serves 5

- 1 can (6-ounces) orange juice concentrate
- 3 tablespoons oil
- 1 tablespoon vinegar
- 1 tablespoon sugar
- 1/4 teaspoon dry mustard
- 1/4 teaspoon salt
- 1/8 teaspoon Tabasco
- 3 cups chicken, cooked and diced
- 1 cup chopped celery
- 1/2 cup olives, sliced
- 1 medium avocado, cut into small chunks
- 1/4 cup slivered almonds, toasted

1. In a blender or a food processor, blend orange juice, oil, vinegar, sugar, dry mustard, salt and Tabasco until smooth.
2. In a salad bowl, combine chicken, celery, olives, avocado and almonds. Stir to combine and serve chilled.

Salad Renaissance | 47

Chicken Salad with Mandarin Dressing

Prep time: 1 hour | Cook time: none | Serves 6

- 2 tablespoons brown sugar
- 5 teaspoons canned mandarin juice
- 2 teaspoons soy sauce
- 1/2 cup canola oil
- 2 tablespoons balsamic vinegar
- 1 head romaine lettuce, torn into bite-sized pieces
- 3 cooked and shredded chicken breasts, boneless skinless
- 1 yellow onion, finely chopped
- 1/4 cup carrot, coarsely grated
- 1/4 cup celery stalks, coarsely grated
- 2 cups dry noodles
- 1/3 cup toasted slivered almonds, chopped

1. Whisk all dressing ingredients until well combined. keep in a refrigerator.
2. In a large salad bowl, combine the lettuce, chicken breasts, onions, noodles, carrots, celery and almonds.
3. Pour the dressing over the salad. Toss to combine ingredients.
4. Serve very chilled.

Greek Chicken Salad

Prep time: 15 minutes | Cook time: 15 minutes | Serves 4

- 1 lb boneless, skinless chicken breasts, grilled and sliced
- 1 cucumber, diced
- 1 cup cherry tomatoes, halved
- 1/2 cup Kalamata olives, pitted and sliced
- 1/2 cup feta cheese, crumbled
- 1/4 cup red onion, thinly sliced
- 1/4 cup fresh parsley, chopped
- Juice of 1 lemon
- 2 tbsp olive oil
- 1 tsp dried oregano
- Salt and pepper to taste

1. In a large bowl, combine grilled and sliced chicken, diced cucumber, crumbled feta cheese, thinly sliced red onion, and chopped fresh parsley.
2. In a small bowl, whisk together lemon juice, olive oil, dried oregano, salt, and pepper to create the dressing.
3. Pour the dressing over the chicken mixture and toss gently to combine.
4. Serve the Greek chicken salad immediately.

Everyday Greek Chicken Salad

Prep time: 10 minutes | Cook time: none | Serves 4

- 1 (8-ounce) bag chopped romaine lettuce
- 3 cups sliced rotisserie chicken
- 1 cup halved cherry tomatoes
- ¾ cup crumbled feta cheese
- ½ cup pitted Kalamata olives
- 2 Roma tomatoes, cut into wedges
- Greek Dressing
- 1 teaspoon Dijon mustard
- ½ teaspoon red pepper flakes

1. In a small bowl, whisk all the ingredients together. Taste for seasoning. Store any leftover dressing in an airtight container in the refrigerator for up to 1 week.
2. Place the lettuce on a platter or in a salad bowl.
3. Top with the chicken, tomatoes, cucumber, feta, olives, tomatoes, and pepperoncini peppers.
4. Drizzle the salad with 3 tablespoons of Greek Dressing. Serve with additional dressing, if desired.

Fajita Chicken and Pepper Salad

Prep time: 30 minutes | Cook time: 5 minutes | Serves 3 or 4

- 1 cup wild rice
- 1 pound chicken breast
- Salt
- ½ teaspoon paprika
- 2 bell peppers (red, yellow, green, or a mix)
- ½ teaspoon sugar
- 6 tablespoons Roasted Poblano Crema
- 1 cup loosely packed fresh cilantro leaves, coarsely chopped

1. Cook the wild rice.
2. While the rice cooks, place the chicken strips on a layer of plastic wrap and with the cumin and paprika.
3. Cut the tenderized chicken and the bell peppers into long strips. Halve the onion crosswise and cut into strips.
4. Remove the skillet from the heat.
5. Divide the rice among three or four plates. Top with the fajita mixture, drizzle with the crema, and garnish with the cilantro. Serve warm.

Mango Avocado Chicken Salad

Prep time: 20 minutes | Cook time: none | Serves 4

- 2 cups cooked and shredded chicken
- 1 ripe mango, diced
- 1 avocado, diced
- 1/4 cup red onion, finely chopped
- 1/4 cup fresh cilantro, chopped
- Juice of 2 limes
- 2 tbsp olive oil
- Salt and pepper to taste
- Mixed salad greens for serving

1. In a large bowl, combine shredded chicken, diced mango, diced avocado, finely chopped red onion, and chopped cilantro.
2. In a small bowl, whisk together lime juice, olive oil, salt, and pepper to create the dressing.
3. Pour the dressing over the chicken mixture and toss gently to combine.
4. Serve the mango avocado chicken salad over a bed of mixed salad greens.

Barbecue Chicken Pizza Salad

Prep time: 15 minutes | Cook time: 5 minutes | Serves 2 or 3

- 1 tablespoon canola oil
- 2 (6-ounce) chicken thighs, cut into bite-size pieces
- ⅓ cup barbecue sauce
- 4 cups torn romaine lettuce
- 2 scallions, green parts only, thinly sliced
- 2 tablespoons pickled red onion or diced red onion
- ⅓ cup shredded white Cheddar cheese

1. Heat the oil in a large skillet over medium-high heat. When hot, add the chicken and cook, stirring occasionally, until cooked through, about 8 minutes.
2. Transfer the chicken to a medium bowl and toss with the barbecue sauce.
3. Divide the romaine between two or three plates. Top with the chicken, scallions, pickled red onion, and cheese. Serve while the chicken is still warm.

Salad Renaissance

Apple and Raisins Chicken Salad

Prep time: 15 minutes | Cook time: none | Serves 4

- 1 tablespoon brown sugar
- 1/3 cup Italian dressing
- 2 tablespoons raisins
- 6 ounces cooked chicken, cut into bite-sized pieces
- 1 apple, cored and thinly sliced
- Chopped almonds for garnish

1. In a small bowl, whisk together brown sugar and Italian dressing.
2. In another medium bowl, combine together raisins, chicken, and apple. Pour dressing mixture over the salad.
3. Stir gently to combine ingredients. Scatter almonds on top and serve chilled.

Grilled Chicken Caesar Salad

Prep time: 15 minutes | Cook time: 15 minutes | Serves 4

- 1 lb boneless, skinless chicken breasts
- Salt and black pepper to taste
- 1 tbsp olive oil
- 1 tsp garlic powder
- 1 tsp dried oregano
- 1/2 cup grated Parmesan cheese
- Caesar dressing (store-bought or homemade)

1. Season chicken breasts with salt, black pepper, garlic powder, and dried oregano.
2. Heat olive oil in a grill pan . Grill chicken for 6-7 minutes per side or until fully cooked.
3. Drizzle Caesar dressing over the top and toss gently to coat.
4. Serve the grilled chicken Caesar salad immediately.

Polynesian Chicken Salad

Prep time: 20 minutes | Cook time: 4 hours 20 minutes | Serves 4

- 1½ pounds boneless, skinless chicken breasts
- 1 can (20 ounces) crushed pineapple in 100% pineapple juice, drained
- 1 green bell pepper, diced
- 1 red onion, finely chopped
- 1 clove garlic, minced
- 2 tablespoons coconut Aminos
- 1 jalapeño, seeded, if desired, and sliced
- lime wedges

1. In a 4-quart slow cooker, combine the chicken, pineapple, bell pepper, onion, garlic, coconut Aminos, salt, and pepper. Turn the chicken to coat. Cover and cook on low for 4 to 5 hours or on high for 2 to 3 hours.
2. Transfer the chicken to a cutting board. Use two forks to shred the chicken, then return to the slow cooker and stir.

Fruity Chicken Chopped Salad

Prep time: 10 minutes | Cook time: 10 minutes | Serves 2

For The Dressing:
- 2 tablespoons fresh orange juice
- 1 tablespoon white wine vinegar
- ⅛ teaspoon salt
- ⅛ teaspoon black pepper

For The Salad:
- 6 cups chopped romaine lettuce
- 1½ cups coarsely chopped cooked chicken
- ¼ cup pomegranate seeds
- ¼ cup coarsely chopped roasted cashews
- 2 green onions, sliced

1. Make the dressing: In a small bowl, whisk together the orange juice, vinegar, olive oil, salt, and pepper.
2. Ma ke the salad: Divide the orange into segments. Drizzle with the dressing and serve.

Curry Chicken Salad

Prep time: 15 minutes | Cook time: 15 minutes | Serves 3 to 4

- ½ cup whole30-compliant mayonnaise or basic mayonnaise
- 1 tablespoon fresh lime juice
- 2 tablespoons fresh cilantro
- 2 teaspoons whole30-compliant curry powder
- ¼ teaspoon salt
- 2 cups diced cooked chicken
- ½ medium apple, diced
- 1 celery stalk, finely diced
- 3 tablespoons finely diced red onion

1. In a medium bowl, stir together the mayonnaise, lime juice, cilantro, curry powder, and salt. Add the chicken, apple, celery, and onion and toss to coat.
2. Fold in the cashews. If desired, top the salad with green onions, cabbage, carrots, and/or additional cashews.

Warm Chicken Salad

Prep time: 20 minutes | Cook time: 4 hours 20 minutes | Serves 4

- 4 green onions
- 2½ pounds bone-in chicken thighs, skin removed
- 3 cloves garlic, minced
- 1 medium red bell pepper, diced
- 2 tablespoons cider vinegar
- ½ cup whole30-compliant mayonnaise
- 1 package (16 ounces) hearts of romaine, chopped

1. Thinly slice the green onions; separate the white bottoms from the green tops. In a 4-quart slow cooker, combine the green onion whites, chicken, broth, and garlic.
2. Let the chicken cool slightly. Remove the chicken from the bones; discard the bones. Use two forks to shred the chicken. Stir the mustard, vinegar, and mayonnaise into the shredded chicken.

Salad Renaissance

Chapter 8

Savory Meat Salads

Walnuts and Bacon Salad Greens

Prep time: 30 minutes | Cook time: none | Serves 4

- 3 tablespoons walnuts, chopped
- 2 bacon slices
- 8 cups gourmet salad greens
- 1/2 teaspoon yellow mustard
- 4 large eggs
- Non-stick cooking spray
- 4 slices French bread baguette, toasted

1. Heat a medium saucepan over medium-high heat and cook the walnuts until lightly browned. Set aside.
2. To make the dressing: In a small mixing bowl, whisk 1 teaspoon reserved drippings, wine vinegar, oil, and mustard.
3. Crack the eggs into custard cups. Microwave the eggs until set. Drain the eggs on paper towels.
4. Drizzle the dressing over the greens mixture. Stir to combine. Divide the salad among serving plates, top with eggs and bread slices and serve.

Blackberry, Ham, and Fig Salad

Prep time: 55 minutes | Cook time: 5 minutes | Serves 2

- 2 cups blackberries, halved
- 1½ teaspoons sugar, divided
- 4 or 5 large fresh figs
- 2 tablespoons unsalted butter
- 4 cups frisée
- ¼ cup Lemon Vinaigrette
- 8 ounces chunk deli ham, diced

1. Place the blackberries in a medium bowl. Sprinkle with ½ teaspoon of sugar and set aside to macerate.
2. Slice the figs lengthwise into ⅛-inch-thick slices.
3. In a large skillet over medium-high melt the butter. Remove the skillet from the heat.
4. While the figs caramelize, toss the frisée with the vinaigrette in a large bowl. Add the ham and toss to combine.
5. Divide the salad between two plates. Top with the blackberries, and figs. Serve warm or at room temperature.

Salad Renaissance | 55

Peach and Pork Salad Rolls

Prep time: 25 minutes | Cook time: none | Serves 6

- 16 (8- to 9-inch) round rice paper sheets
- 2 medium peaches, peeled and thinly sliced
- 16 butter lettuce leaves
- 1 lb. roasted pork, shredded
- 1 apple, peeled and thinly sliced
- 1 teaspoon salt
- 1/4 teaspoon black pepper
- 2 tablespoons fresh basil leaves
- 2 tablespoons fresh mint leaves

1. Pour hot water into a large dish. Soak 1 rice paper sheet in hot water for 10 to 15 seconds. Repeat the process with remaining rice papers.
2. Place 2 slices of peach on the rice paper. 1 to 2 avocado slice, 2 to 3 pork pieces, 3 apple strips. Sprinkle with seasonings.
3. Fold the bottom edge of your rice paper sheet over the filling. Then roll up the stuffed rice paper sheet.
4. Repeat this procedure with remaining ingredients. Cut each roll into halves.

Turkey and Cranberry Quinoa Salad

Prep time: 20 minutes | Cook time: 15 minutes | Serves 4

- 1 cup quinoa, cooked
- 1 lb turkey breast, cooked and diced
- 1/4 cup pecans, chopped
- 1/4 cup green onions, sliced
- 1/4 cup feta cheese, crumbled
- 2 tbsp olive oil
- 1 tbsp Dijon mustard
- 1 tbsp apple cider vinegar
- Salt and pepper to taste

1. In a large bowl, combine cooked quinoa, diced turkey breast, dried cranberries, chopped pecans, sliced green onions, and crumbled feta cheese.
2. In a small bowl, whisk together olive oil, Dijon mustard, honey, apple cider vinegar, salt, and pepper to create the dressing.
3. Pour the dressing over the quinoa mixture and toss gently to combine.
4. Serve the turkey and cranberry quinoa salad at room temperature or chilled.

Sausage Onion Salad

Prep time: 30 minutes | Cook time: none | Serves 4

- 1/2 pound Knockwurst, cooked
- 2 pickles, sliced
- 1 onion, chopped
- 3 tablespoons vinegar
- 1 tablespoon mustard
- 2 tablespoons olive oil
- 1/2 teaspoon salt
- 1/4 teaspoon black pepper
- 1 teaspoon sugar
- 1 tablespoon fresh parsley, chopped

1. Cut the knockwurst into bite-sized cubes. Add pickles and onion. Stir to combine
2. Mix vinegar together with mustard and olive oil. Add salt, pepper, and sugar. Stir to combine ingredients.
3. Stir in the cubed knockwurst, pickles, and onions.
4. Garnish with parsley and serve.

Hawaiian Luau Pork Salad

Prep time: 10 minutes | Cook time: none | Serves 4

- 1 (16-ounce) package precooked pulled pork
- 2 cups coleslaw mix
- 1 (8-ounce) can pineapple tidbits
- Sweet Chili Pineapple Dressing
- ¼ cup vegetable oil
- 3 tablespoons juice from the pineapple tidbits
- 2 tablespoons sweet chili sauce
- ½ teaspoon kosher salt
- ½ teaspoon garlic powder

1. In a small bowl, whisk all the ingredients together. Taste for seasoning. Store any leftover dressing in an airtight container in the refrigerator for up to 1 week.
2. Heat the pulled pork according to package instructions.
3. In a large bowl, toss all the ingredients together with 3 tablespoons of Sweet Chili Pineapple Dressing. Taste and add more dressing, if desired.

Salad Renaissance

Cold Lamb Salad

Prep time: 20 minutes | **Cook time:** none | **Serves 6**

- Cold roast lamb
- 2 lettuces
- 1 large tomato, sliced
- 12 capers
- Salad dressing
- Salt to taste
- Black pepper to taste
- 2 eggs

1. Cut the lamb into bite-sized chunks. Arrange the lamb in a serving bowl.
2. Place lettuces, tomato and capers and then pour in salad dressing. Add salt and pepper and adjust seasonings.
3. Place hard-boiled eggs on top and serve chilled.

Steak and Blue Cheese Salad

Prep time: 15 minutes | **Cook time:** 10 minutes | **Serves 4**

- 1 lb flank steak
- Salt and black pepper to taste
- 1 tsp smoked paprika
- 8 cups mixed salad greens
- 1/2 red onion, thinly sliced
- 1/2 cup blue cheese, crumbled
- Balsamic vinaigrette dressing

1. Season the flank steak with salt, black pepper, garlic powder, and smoked paprika.
2. Heat olive oil in a skillet medium-high heat.
3. In a large salad bowl, combine mixed greens, halved cherry tomatoes, thinly sliced red onion, and crumbled blue cheese.
4. Serve the steak and blue cheese salad immediately.

Hot Beef and Broccoli Salad

Prep time: 15 minutes | Cook time: 30 minutes | Serves 4

- 1 pound boneless beef sirloin steak or stir-fry meat
- ½ teaspoon salt
- ¼ teaspoon black pepper
- 2 teaspoons grated lemon zest
- 6 tablespoons whole30-compliant lemon-garlic dressing
- 3 cups broccoli florets
- ¼ cup snipped fresh chives

1. Thinly slice the meat across the grain into bite-size pieces and season both sides with the salt, pepper, and lemon zest. In a medium bowl, toss the meat with 2 tablespoons of the dressing.
2. In a large bowl, toss the greens with the remaining 1 tablespoon dressing. Serve the meat and vegetables over the greens. Sprinkle the salad with the snipped chives.

Beef Taco Salad

Prep time: 15 minutes | Cook time: 2 hours 15 minutes | Serves 6

- 1½ pounds lean ground beef
- 1 medium white onion, diced
- 2 cloves garlic, minced
- 2 anaheim Chile peppers, seeded and finely chopped
- 1 tablespoon ground cumin
- 1 teaspoon dried oregano
- 1 teaspoon chili powder
- 1 teaspoon salt
- 1 teaspoon black pepper
- 1 bag (10 ounces) chopped romaine or 1 head romaine lettuce, chopped
- 2 limes, cut into wedges

1. Cover and cook on high for 2 hours.
2. Serve the taco meat on top of the chopped lettuce. Top servings with green onions, tomatoes, and jalapeños, along with salsa and cilantro, if desired. Serve with the lime wedges.

Salad Renaissance | 59

Sizzling Pork Greek Salad

Prep time: 10 minutes | Cook time: 20 minutes | Serves 4

For The Pork:
- 1 pound ground pork
- 1 teaspoon greek seasoning
- ½ cup thinly sliced red onion
- ½ cup sliced pitted kalamata olives

For The Salad:
- 3 tablespoons red wine vinegar
- 1 or 2 cloves garlic, minced
- ¼ cup extra-virgin olive oil
- 1 medium cucumber, chopped

1. Cook the pork: In a large nonstick skillet, cook the pork and Greek seasoning over medium-high heat, stirring occasionally, until browned and crispy, 6 to 8 minutes. Turn off the heat. Stir in the red onion and olives. Let stand for 2 minutes to soften the onion.
2. Layer the lettuce, cucumber, and pork in bowls. Drizzle with the dressing and serve.

Easy Beef Salad Wraps

Prep time: 10 minutes | Cook time: 10 minutes | Serves 2

- ¼ cup whole30-compliant mayonnaise or basic mayonnaise
- 1 clove garlic, minced
- 1 tablespoon chopped fresh basil
- ½ teaspoon grated lemon zest
- 1 teaspoon fresh lemon juice
- 12 large Bibb lettuce leaves
- 8 ounces whole30-compliant sliced roast beef, cut into ½-inch strips
- 1 medium avocado, halved, pitted, peeled, and diced
- 1 cup quartered or halved cherry tomatoes

1. Make the dressing: In a small bowl, stir together the mayonnaise, garlic, basil, and lemon zest and juice.
2. Arrange the lettuce leaves on two serving plates. Divide the roast beef strips, avocado, and tomatoes among the leaves. Drizzle with the dressing and serve.

Appendix 1 Measurement Conversion Chart

Volume Equivalents (Dry)	
US STANDARD	METRIC (APPROXIMATE)
1/8 teaspoon	0.5 mL
1/4 teaspoon	1 mL
1/2 teaspoon	2 mL
3/4 teaspoon	4 mL
1 teaspoon	5 mL
1 tablespoon	15 mL
1/4 cup	59 mL
1/2 cup	118 mL
3/4 cup	177 mL
1 cup	235 mL
2 cups	475 mL
3 cups	700 mL
4 cups	1 L

Volume Equivalents (Liquid)		
US STANDARD	US STANDARD (OUNCES)	METRIC (APPROXIMATE)
2 tablespoons	1 fl.oz.	30 mL
1/4 cup	2 fl.oz.	60 mL
1/2 cup	4 fl.oz.	120 mL
1 cup	8 fl.oz.	240 mL
1 1/2 cup	12 fl.oz.	355 mL
2 cups or 1 pint	16 fl.oz.	475 mL
4 cups or 1 quart	32 fl.oz.	1 L
1 gallon	128 fl.oz.	4 L

Temperatures Equivalents	
FAHRENHEIT(F)	CELSIUS(C) APPROXIMATE
225 °F	107 °C
250 °F	120 ° °C
275 °F	135 °C
300 °F	150 °C
325 °F	160 °C
350 °F	180 °C
375 °F	190 °C
400 °F	205 °C
425 °F	220 °C
450 °F	235 °C
475 °F	245 °C
500 °F	260 °C

Weight Equivalents	
US STANDARD	METRIC (APPROXIMATE)
1 ounce	28 g
2 ounces	57 g
5 ounces	142 g
10 ounces	284 g
15 ounces	425 g
16 ounces (1 pound)	455 g
1.5 pounds	680 g
2 pounds	907 g

Appendix 2 The Dirty Dozen and Clean Fifteen

The Environmental Working Group (EWG) is a nonprofit, nonpartisan organization dedicated to protecting human health and the environment Its mission is to empower people to live healthier lives in a healthier environment. This organization publishes an annual list of the twelve kinds of produce, in sequence, that have the highest amount of pesticide residue-the Dirty Dozen-as well as a list of the fifteen kinds ofproduce that have the least amount of pesticide residue-the Clean Fifteen.

THE DIRTY DOZEN

The 2016 Dirty Dozen includes the following produce. These are considered among the year's most important produce to buy organic:

Strawberries	Spinach
Apples	Tomatoes
Nectarines	Bell peppers
Peaches	Cherry tomatoes
Celery	Cucumbers
Grapes	Kale/collard greens
Cherries	Hot peppers

The Dirty Dozen list contains two additional itemskale/collard greens and hot peppers-because they tend to contain trace levels of highly hazardous pesticides.

THE CLEAN FIFTEEN

The least critical to buy organically are the Clean Fifteen list. The following are on the 2016 list:

Avocados	Papayas
Corn	Kiw
Pineapples	Eggplant
Cabbage	Honeydew
Sweet peas	Grapefruit
Onions	Cantaloupe
Asparagus	Cauliflower
Mangos	

Some of the sweet corn sold in the United States are made from genetically engineered (GE) seedstock. Buy organic varieties of these crops to avoid GE produce.

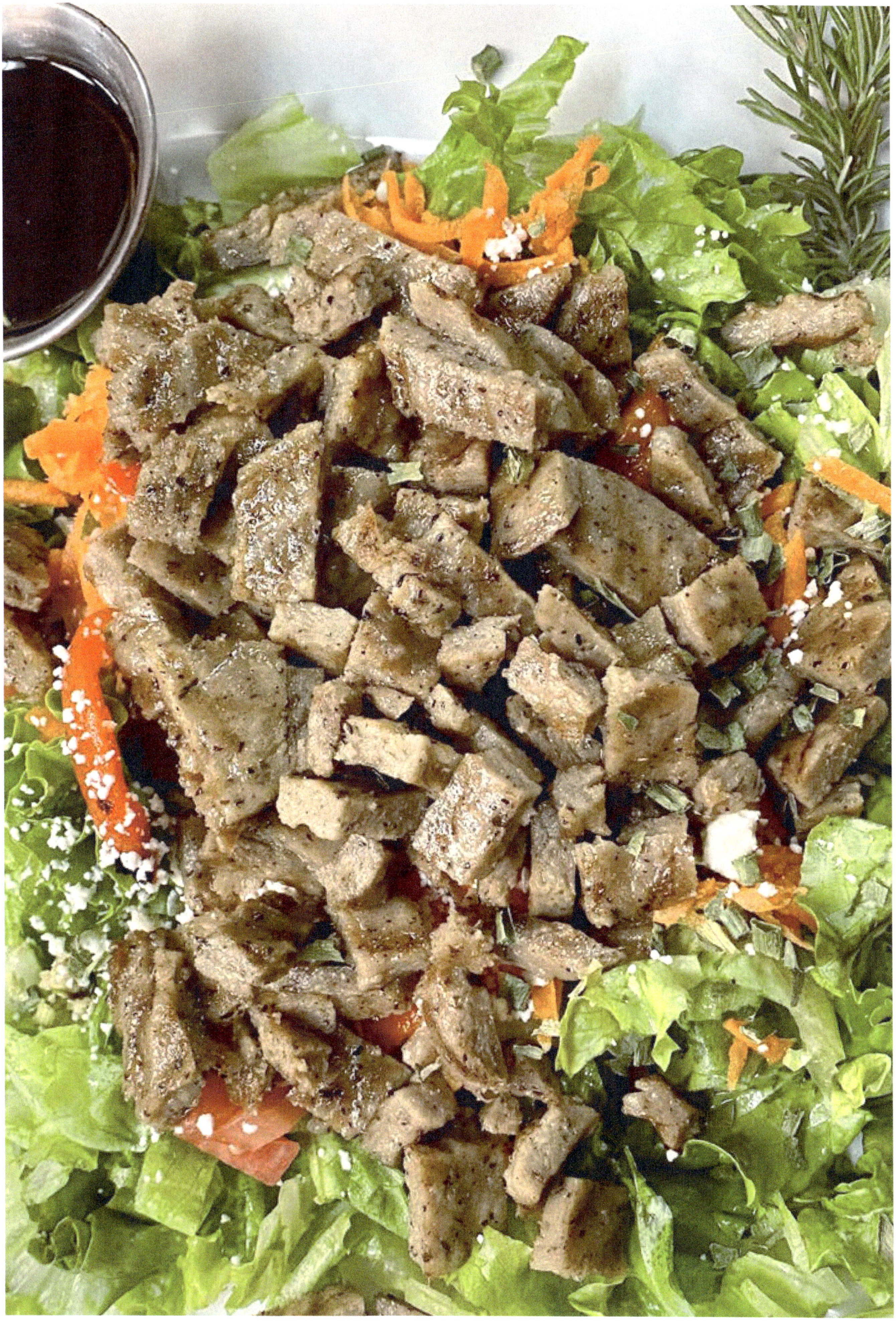

Appendix 3 Index

A

adobo sauce 40
almonds 18, 31, 47, 48, 51
apple 9, 33, 51, 56
arugula 41
asparagus 47
avocado 11, 34, 43, 47, 50, 56

B

bacon 25, 55
Balsamic 10, 23, 58
basil 9, 18, 27, 56
BBQ sauce 33
bell peppers 27, 49
blackberries 55
black pepper 10, 13, 17, 18, 20, 23, 24, 25, 26
blue cheese 58
breadcrumbs 47

C

carrot 20, 35, 39, 48
celery stalks 48
Cheddar cheese 23, 50
chicken 47, 48, 49, 50, 51
chives 12, 26
cilantro 11, 31, 33, 34, 43, 49, 50
coarsely 18, 48, 49
cucumber 16, 18, 20, 26, 27, 31, 33, 48, 49

D

Dijon mustard 10, 11, 12, 19, 23, 27, 34, 39, 49, 56

dry mustard 26, 47

E

eggs 17, 25, 26, 31, 34, 35, 40, 41, 42, 55, 58
extra-virgin olive oil 10, 13, 17, 18, 19, 20, 40, 41, 42

F

feta cheese 16, 23, 27, 39, 42, 48, 49, 56

G

garlic 9, 10, 11, 12, 13, 17, 18, 24, 27, 32, 33
garlic powder 27, 33, 51, 57, 58
granulated sugar 27
grapes 19, 23, 31

H

honey 9, 13, 20, 56

I

Italian dressing 23, 51

J

julienne grated 20

K

kosher salt 18, 40, 57

64 | *Salad Renaissance*

L

leeks 17, 25, 27, 39, 47
Lemon Vinaigrette 13, 40, 55
lettuces 58
lime 11, 16, 18, 34, 50

M

macaroni 26
mango 50
maple syrup 10, 35
Mayonnaise 41
mint 56

O

oil 9, 10, 11, 12, 13, 16, 17, 18, 19, 20, 24
olive 9, 10, 11, 12, 13, 16, 17, 18, 19, 20
onion 12, 16, 18, 19, 20, 24, 33
oregano 10, 16, 18, 27, 41, 48, 51

P

papaya 20
paprika 17, 18, 24, 33, 49, 58
Parmesan 25, 43, 47, 51
parsley 10, 16, 17, 24, 27, 34, 42, 47, 48, 57
peas 17, 33, 39
pineapple 57
pork 26, 56, 57

Q

quinoa 33, 39, 56

R

raisins 19, 51
raw tahini 12

red onion 16, 18, 19, 33, 34, 39, 43, 48, 50, 58
rice 10, 13, 23, 26, 27, 31, 32, 47, 49, 56
romaine lettuce 42, 48, 49, 50

S

Salt 10, 11, 12, 17, 24, 25, 33, 34, 39, 40
scallions 24, 26, 27, 31, 32, 41, 50
sea salt 16, 17, 31
sesame seeds 12, 16, 18, 20, 35
shrimp 39, 40, 42, 43
spinach 18, 23, 27, 31, 47
sugar 27, 47, 48, 49, 51, 55, 57

T

Tabasco 35, 47
Thai Chili 32
tofu 26, 31, 32, 33, 35
tomato 58
tuna 41, 42

V

vinegar 9, 10, 13, 19, 23, 26, 31, 32, 33, 34, 47, 48, 55, 56, 57

W

walnuts 19, 25, 33, 47, 55
white vinegar 34

Y

yogurt 11, 12, 39

Z

zucchini 12, 27, 33

Salad Renaissance | 65

Elizabeth E. Wright

Printed in Great Britain
by Amazon